Alma and Faith

written by Tiffany Thomas
illustrated by Nikki Casassa

CFI • An imprint of Cedar Fort, Inc. • Springville, Utah

HARD WORDS:
humble, faith, ground, believe

PARENT TIP: Encourage your child to read aloud to other people, such as siblings and grandparents.

Alma the Younger
is now the prophet.

He teaches the bad Nephites.

They do not want to listen.
They are proud.

Some are humble and
want to hear Alma.

Alma teaches
them about faith.

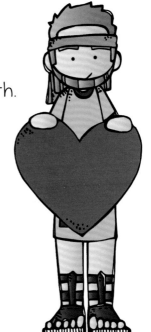

Faith is when you
trust God and believe.

You cannot know or see faith.

Alma says faith is like a seed.

You put it in the ground and water it.

You have faith the seed will grow.

Make your
faith grow by
obeying God.

The end.

ISBN 13: 978-1-4621-4337-5

Published by CFI, an imprint of Cedar Fort, Inc. • 2373 W. 700 S., Suite 100, Springville, UT 84663
Distributed by Cedar Fort, Inc., www.cedarfort.com

Cover design and interior layout design by Shawnda T. Craig
Cover design © 2022 Cedar Fort, Inc.
Printed in China • Printed on acid-free paper
10 9 8 7 6 5 4 3 2 1